MEMORIES
of My Daddy

A Child's Memory Book After the Loss of a Father

KATHRYN E. ROBINETT

Kat Rob Books Publishing

This book is

Given to

By

In Memory of

----

on

In Loving Memory of
Sandra Alice Kangeter Corson
(affectionately known as Bubba)
1945-1983

Dedication

To my Mom,

Even though I only had six years on Earth with you,
I am so blessed to know that I will get to spend eternity with you.
This book is in your honor.
I will always love you,
Katie Caboose

To any child who has lost a parent,

You are not alone. I can relate to the pain you are experiencing, but no one will understand your story and your pain because your story is unique to you. I hurt with you, but be reminded that there is joy beyond the pain. Please take the time to grieve, take the time to remember, and take the time to laugh. Your grief will come in waves, and when it does, it is okay to feel ALL the emotions. Write down everything you are feeling and experiencing and don't bottle anything up. It's okay to be sad, and it's okay to be happy.
You will find your balance, but give yourself permission to feel deeply.

My biggest desire for you is to keep your loved one's memory alive as you grow older. Write down everything so that you may never forget. I wrote this for you so that you will have a way to keep your loved one's memory alive for years to come. I hope this helps you through your grieving process.
Love,
Kathryn

Acknowledgments

To my family,
Dad, San, Crissy, Jamie, Matthew, Stephen,
David, Madilyn, Logan, Gabriel, & Sophie Rose,
Without each of you, I wouldn't be where I am and who I am. God knew
that each of you are exactly what I needed in my life. He gave me each of
you for a purpose, and I'm so grateful for every one of you.
I love you,
Katie/Boose/Kathryn/Momma

San,
You stepped into a role that very few could handle. We had our rocky
"growing up" years (as you say), but you forged through. You've raised me
since I was 7, and you've always called me your daughter, which has never
gone unnoticed. Your excitement when I told you about this book, fueled me
to start the process, for which I am so incredibly grateful.
From the bottom of my heart,
thank you for loving me, for being my best friend, and for being my Mom.
Love,
Your Daughter

To countless others,
I can't possibly attempt to name everyone that helped me to create these
books: people who prayed for me, gave me ideas and prompts, advised me,
proofread for me, encouraged me, loved me and overall supported me and
the vision for these books. Not only do I sincerely thank you for helping me
turn my tragedy into hope for others, but on behalf of all the people these
books will help, you are appreciated, and you are a blessing.
Kathryn

Special Acknowledgements

Illustrations

Not only did my husband and children encourage me, support me,
and give me advice throughout this process,
they also wanted to help with my book in a special way.
Each of them have added illustrations that they personally drew throughout the
book. We hope that you enjoy that special touch from our family to yours.

Logo and Editing

To Tim and Sandi,
Your humbleness, generosity, commitment to Christ, and desire to serve others
are an inspiration to me. Thank you for your selfless contributions.
With much love and appreciation,
Kathryn

Everything

To the Creator of All,
Thank you, God, for allowing me to find purpose behind my pain, for sending joy
after the sorrow, for constantly showing me where to find the good in ALL
circumstances, and most importantly, for sending Your Son to die for us. Because
of Your great sacrifice, I will be reunited with Mom one day.
Thank you, Jesus.

"And we know that in all things God works for the good of those who love Him,
who have been called according to His purpose" Romans 8:28 (NIV).

My Story

This book is inspired by the sudden loss of my Mom when I was six-years-old. I have absolutely no memories of her. Due to the shock of her death, I mentally blocked any memories that potentially could have stayed with me. Many times over the years, I wished that someone would have written some things down for me -- things that could have helped me to remember who she was, what she loved, what she didn't love, and so much more. I especially wish someone had written down MY memories for me so that I would not have forgotten them. As I grew older, I would have known those were my own thoughts and not things someone told me.

Every time I hear of a child losing a parent, I try to recommend that family members sit down and ask the child some questions to get his/her memories down on paper. I began to search for a memory book to give as a gift. I saw that there was a need for a memory book written from the point of view of the child.

This became the inspiration for these memory books. They contain prompts with simple fill-in-the blanks, short answer questions, and open-ended questions. The child can fill it out on their own or with the help of an adult, or some of both. There also is a section in the back for other people to add their memories as well.

My hope is the child can get their memories documented while they are fresh. Their personal memories will stay in their own words so that they never have to wonder who their loved one was and what their loved one meant to them.

I would love to hear from you -- to hear your story as well as suggestions for future Memory Books and/or ideas for prompts.

Please email me directly at KatRobBooks@gmail.com.
Find more information at www.KatRobBooks.com.

How to Use This Journal

- Fill out as soon as possible after death while memories are fresh, but feel free to add more memories/thoughts as you wish. Don't feel like it all has to be done at one time.
- Use the pages to add photos, samples of writing, etc.
- There is a section for others to add in their memories, too. Don't skip this part. You'll enjoy reading stories from others!
- Not all prompts will pertain to you. Just skip those or write something different in that space.
- Some prompts are repeated because asking in different ways elicits a different response. If you have the same answer, come back to it later and see if you have a different response.
- Not all of the prompts included are positive. It's important that we remember our loved one isn't some perfect image that we have to live up to. As a child of parent-loss, people have told me things that my Mom loved to say/do, etc, but there also is value in knowing what she didn't like as well. It would have helped me to know her more as a whole person, so I hope you don't skip over those parts.

For adults helping a young child:
- When completing this for a baby or toddler, try to write in as many things possible. If others had those experiences instead of the child, write those in but mark whose memory it was so if the child wants to know more details, he/she will know who to ask.
- Try to write as much as possible in the child's words--exact quotes. It'll make it much more genuine for the child as he/she ages.
- Please keep this book in a safe spot for him/her and pull it out whenever needed. People go through many stages of grief and when they go through the anger stage (which can happen multiple times and at any age), he/she may destroy parts of this book due to grief. Please keep this safe until he/she is older.

*Disclaimer: I am not a therapist, nor have I studied grief/counseling/etc, but I do have my personal thoughts and experience dealing with death. Please use the advice as you wish but know that it didn't come from a licensed therapist.

All About Me!

My full name is

But everyone calls me

I am

years old.

My birthday is

My brothers/sisters are

This is what I look like

All About Daddy!

My Daddy's full name is

But I always call him

Daddy's job was

My Daddy's parents are

My Daddy's siblings are

When Daddy died, he was _____ years old,
and I was _____ years old.

THIS IS THE STORY
OF HOW MY DADDY DIED:

~HONOR~

What are some ways you could honor your Dad?
Think of things he loved or charities he cared about.
Talk with your family to get more ideas.

Then pick one idea to become a tradition to do every year on
the anniversary of his death, and write it on the next page.
You could do this by yourself, with family and friends, or
even invite the whole community.

Here are some ideas to get you started:
- Organize a fundraiser for his favorite charity.
- Cook a special meal that was his favorite.
- Go to a special event or place that he loved.
- Light candles/lanterns.
- Have a Day of Kindness or Pay It Forward Day.

- _____
- _____
- _____
- _____
- _____

Every year on the anniversary of Dad's death, I want to

_____

_____

I want to do this

☐ all by myself

☐ with friends and family

☐ include the whole community

Other things I need to do to make this happen:

- _____

- _____

- _____

- _____

I think Daddy would love this tradition because

_____

_____

Do you have an animal or special item that when you see it, it reminds you of Daddy?

If you don't, pay attention and see if you begin to notice something that is often around when you are thinking of him.

A _____ reminds me of my Daddy because

_____

_____

Draw or glue a photo of it here:

It's OKAY to feel sad and happy at the same time!

You may feel HAPPY that you won your soccer game but SAD your Daddy wasn't there to see it.

You could feel HAPPY that you met new friends but SAD that your Daddy doesn't get to meet them.

Those feelings are very NORMAL! When you feel that way, TALK to someone about it. Talking is a great way to sort through all your

BIG FEELINGS!

You also can write in this journal or in another journal. Writing and drawing also help us to understand our big feelings.

Who are the people that you can **TALK** to when you are feeling sad?

Put their names in the talking bubbles.
Add their phone numbers if you have them, too!

Date:_____

Today, I feel **HAPPY** because _____

_____, but I also feel **SAD**

because_____

_____

Date:_____

Today, I feel **HAPPY** because _____

_____, but I also feel **SAD**

because_____

_____

Date:_____

Today, I feel **HAPPY** because _____

_____, but I also feel **SAD**

because_____

_____

Date:_____

Today, I feel **HAPPY** because _____

_____, but I also feel **SAD**

because_____

_____

Date:_____

Today, I feel **HAPPY** because _____

_____, but I also feel **SAD**

because_____

_____

Date:_____

Today, I feel **HAPPY** because _____

_____, but I also feel **SAD**

because_____

_____

Date:_____

Today, I feel **HAPPY** because _____
_____, but I also feel **SAD**

because_____
_____

Date:_____

Today, I feel **HAPPY** because _____
_____, but I also feel **SAD**

because_____
_____

Date:_____

Today, I feel **HAPPY** because _____
_____, but I also feel **SAD**

because_____
_____

Daddy as a Little Boy

Daddy's favorite
childhood vacation was

_____

_____

_____

_____

_____

_____

When Daddy was a
little boy, he wanted to
be a

_____

when he grew up.

When Daddy was a little boy, he was

_____

_____

_____

Daddy said
that his parents

_____

_____

_____

A funny story about Daddy
when he was a little boy is

_____

_____

_____

_____

Daddy's nickname was _____.

He got the nickname because _____

_____

_____

Daddy got into trouble as a little boy for _____

_____

_____

Daddy as a Little Boy

Draw or glue some photos of when Daddy was a little boy.
Make sure you put a date with each picture.

Daddy as a Little Boy

Daddy's
Favorites & Least Favorites

Favorite   Least Favorite

_____ COLOR _____

_____ FOOD _____

_____ DRINK _____

_____ RESTAURANT _____

_____ PLACE _____

_____ TV SHOW _____

_____ MOVIE _____

_____ THING TO SAY _____

_____ BIBLE VERSE _____

_____ THING TO COOK _____

_____ TEAM _____

_____ SONG _____

Favorite Places

Daddy's favorite place to

~visit was _____

~be in the whole world was _____

~be in our hometown was _____

~be in our home was _____

~go out to eat was _____

~get fast food was _____

~get dessert or a treat was _____

~get coffee was _____

~shop was _____

~get groceries was _____

~go for fun was _____

~take the whole family was _____

~go by himself was _____

~go with friends was _____

~go with _____ was _____

My Best Daddy

My Daddy was the best because

The best advice he gave me was

One time I was very sad because

and Daddy helped me feel better by

Daddy and Me

Things Daddy and I did together
(put a ☆ next to your favorites!)

_____

_____

_____

_____

_____

_____

_____

_____

_____

Vacations/Trips with Daddy
(put a ☆ next to your favorites!)

_____

_____

_____

_____

_____

_____

_____

_____

_____

A nickname or silly name that
Daddy would call me was

Personality traits I inherited
from Daddy are

Daddy and Me

Draw or glue pictures of you and your Daddy doing your favorite things together.

Daddy and Me

Draw or glue pictures of you and your Daddy together.

TV SHOWS

Daddy loved to watch _____ on tv.

We loved to watch _____ together.

His other favorite shows were

_____   _____

_____   _____

GAMES

Daddy loved to play _____ with me.

He loved to play _____ with friends.

Other games he loved were

_____   _____

_____   _____

HOBBIES

Daddy's favorite hobbies were

_____   _____

Old Wives Tales he always believed were
(Old Wives Tales are beliefs that have been passed down from people who have lived before them.)

_____

_____

_____

Whenever I got hurt, he had a special way to make my boo-boos better by

_____

_____

Daddy taught me

_____

_____

_____

_____

_____

_____

MY FUNNY DADDY

Daddy made me laugh when he

One time, Daddy and I laughed
so hard when

Ha Ha!!

His favorite joke was

_____

_____

_____

_____

_____

Daddy's funniest prank was

_____

_____

_____

_____

Something silly that Daddy would always do was

_____

_____

_____

_____

HOW DADDY LOOKED

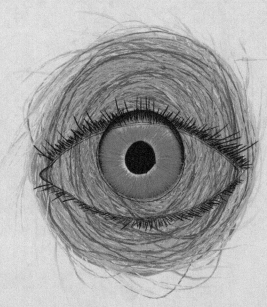

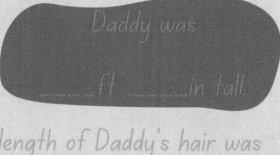
Daddy was
_____ft _____in tall.

The length of Daddy's hair was

☐ bald

☐ very short like military cut

☐ short sides but longer on top

☐ long (to ears or shoulders)

☐ very long (past shouders)

Daddy's eye color was

_____.

The color of his hair was

_____

His facial hair was

_____

An expression that Daddy always made was

_____

Draw the face to look just like Daddy.

My Daddy

Draw or glue some recent photos of Daddy.

Daddy's smile was

Daddy's hands were

Tips to help you think:

Did he like to sit or stand (crisscross, legs to the side, hands on hips, one-legged like a flamingo) a certain way? It's okay if you don't have an answer. You can always ask family members to help.

Daddy's feet were

Daddy always liked to sit

Daddy always liked to stand

Daddy danced like

Favorite Clothes

Fashion

his favorite outfit was

_____

_____

_____

Pajamas

When Daddy went to bed, he liked to wear

_____

Daddy had a special
_____
(shirt/tie/sweater/etc.)
that he cherished because

_____

_____

_____

_____

Shoes

Daddy wore size _____ shoe.

He had around _____ pairs of shoes.

His favorite shoes were

_____.

Daddy's Handwriting

Daddy liked to write in
(circle one)

print

cursive

mix of both.

She had a special way to write

Daddy liked to write with a special

He liked to write
(in a journal, notes, cards, etc.)

Daddy's Special Jewelry

List any rings, bracelets, necklaces, or earrings that
Daddy loved to wear or ones that were very special.
Try to add as many details as you can, and ask family members to help.

_____

_____

_____

Handwriting Samples

Glue samples of Daddy's handwriting to this page.

Hidden Treasures

He liked to hide or put things in strange places, like

Things you could always find in Daddy's pockets were

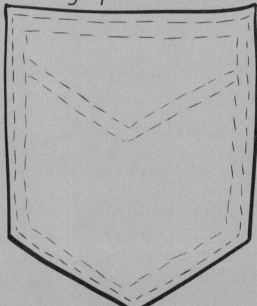

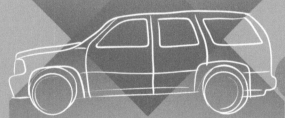

Things you could always find in Daddy's car were

Items that were always displayed in Daddy's house were
(pictures, artwork, collections, etc.)

HOW DADDY SOUNDED

His voice sounded like

His laugh sounded like

Something he always said incorrectly was

A recording of him is saved

Something he always said that he thought was so funny was

THINGS DADDY SAID

I loved it when Daddy said, "_____

_____."

My favorite thing he said was "_____

_____."

When he woke me up in the mornings, he always said, "_____

_____."

My Daddy always said, "_____

_____."

Daddy always told me to "_____

_____."

When Daddy put me to bed, he always said, "_____

_____

_____"

★★★ Best Advice ★★★

If you don't know what to write, ask others what advice he gave them.

The best advice he gave me was _____

_____.

The best advice he gave me about school was _____

_____.

The best advice he gave me about friends was _____

_____.

The best advice he gave me about growing up was _____

_____

_____.

If he could give me advice right now, he would say _____

_____

_____.

Music & Daddy

The type of music Daddy listened to was

He loved music by the artist

His favorite song was

He loved to sing

A special song that he sang just for me was

One time, Daddy started singing

What is the song that reminds you the most of Daddy?

Tape or write the lyrics below.

....

by

....

Daddy smelled like _____.

He loved the smell of _____.

His house always smelled like _____.

Daddy's cologne was called _____.

He used _____ laundry detergent and _____ soap.

Whenever I smell _____, I will always think of Daddy because

_____.

SMELLS

All About Food

Daddy's favorite meal was
(circle one)

breakfast   lunch   dinner

F
O
O
D

D
A
D
D
Y

L
O
V
E
D

_____
Dinner

_____
Lunch

_____
Breakfast

_____
Vegetable

_____
Fruit

_____
Meat

_____
Drink

_____
Candy

_____
Special Treat

_____
Dessert

_____
Snack

_____
Gum

Daddy's favorite thing to order at _____ was

_____

Grillin' & Cookin'

When Daddy cooked, he would always

----------------------------------.

The meal he made the most was

----------------------------------.

My favorite food Daddy made for me was

----------------------------------.

My favorite food I made with Daddy was

----------------------------------.

A food he made when I wasn't feeling well was

----------------------------------.

Random things Daddy did while cooking were

----------------------------------.

Daddy liked his steak
(cirle one)

rare   medium rare

medium   medium well

well done

Things Daddy taught me about cooking were

Dad's Recipes

Write or glue some recipes below.

Dad's Special Meals

Write or glue some meals below.

Holiday Traditions

Write as many details as you can for each holiday.

New Year's Eve & Day

Valentine's Day

St. Patrick's Day

Easter

Holiday Traditions

Write as many details as you can for each holiday.

Mother's Day

Father's Day

First/Last Day of School

4th of July

Holiday Traditions

Write as many details as you can for each holiday.

Halloween

Thanksgiving
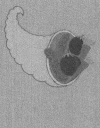

Christmas/ Hanukkah

Birthdays

Other Holiday Traditions

Other Traditions

Do you have any other family traditions?
Things you do every day, week, month, or year?
Use this space to write in any traditions. Ask family members to help!

_____

_____

_____

_____

_____

_____

_____

_____

_____

_____

Happy

Silly

Sad

Funny

_____

_____

Random Memories

So Proud...

Reasons why I'm proud that he was my Daddy are

_____

_____

_____

_____

Reasons why Daddy was proud I am his child are

_____

_____

_____

_____

_____

Things I've done after he passed that I know he's proud of me are

(Each time you have an accomplishment over the years, add it here and
know that your Dad is so proud of you!)

_____

_____

_____

_____

_____

_____

_____

_____

_____

_____

_____

_____

_____

Memories From Others

You can learn more about your **DADDY** by **MEMORIES** from others who also knew him.

Find some of **DADDY'S** friends, co-workers, or family members, and ask them about him.

There are **TWO** ways to record their **MEMORIES.**

You can use the **INTERVIEW** pages, or you can have them write their own **MEMORIES** on the spaces at the back of the book.

Some people may prefer to answer the **QUESTIONS,** while others may prefer to **WRITE** out a story.

Try to get as many pages completed so that you will **ALWAYS KNOW HOW MUCH HE MEANT TO OTHER PEOPLE.**

Memories From Others - Interview

1. What is your name? _____

2. How did you know my Daddy? _____

3. How long have you known him? _____

4. What is one word you would use to describe him? _____

5. What was your favorite thing about my Daddy? _____

6. Did my Daddy ever teach you anything? _____

_____

7. Did my Daddy ever tell you anything about me? _____

_____

8. What is something you will always remember about him? ____

_____

9. If there was something Daddy would want me to always remember, what would it be?

_____

_____

10. Do you have a good story about Daddy? _____

_____

_____

_____

Memories From Others - Interview

1. What is your name? _____

2. How did you know my Daddy?_____

3. How long have you known him? _____

4. What is one word you would use to describe him? _____

5. What was your favorite thing about my Daddy? _____

6. Did my Daddy ever teach you anything?_____

_____

7. Did my Daddy ever tell you anything about me? _____

_____

8. What is something you will always remember about him?_____

_____

9. If there was something Daddy would want me to always remember, what would it be?

_____

_____

10. Do you have a good story about Daddy? _____

_____

_____

_____

Memories From Others - Interview

1. What is your name? _____

2. How did you know my Daddy?_____

3. How long have you known him? _____

4. What is one word you would use to describe him? _____

5. What was your favorite thing about my Daddy? _____

6. Did my Daddy ever teach you anything?_____

_____

7. Did my Daddy ever tell you anything about me? _____

_____

8. What is something you will always remember about him?_____

_____

9. If there was something Daddy would want me to always remember, what would it be?

_____

_____

10. Do you have a good story about Daddy? _____

_____

_____

_____

Memories From Others - Interview

1. What is your name? _____

2. How did you know my Daddy?_____

3. How long have you known him? _____

4. What is one word you would use to describe him? _____

5. What was your favorite thing about my Daddy? _____

6. Did my Daddy ever teach you anything?_____

_____

7. Did my Daddy ever tell you anything about me? _____

_____

8. What is something you will always remember about him?_____

_____

9. If there was something Daddy would want me to always remember, what would it be?

_____

_____

10. Do you have a good story about Daddy? _____

_____

_____

_____

Memories From Others - Interview

1. What is your name? _____

2. How did you know my Daddy? _____

3. How long have you known him? _____

4. What is one word you would use to describe him? _____

5. What was your favorite thing about my Daddy? _____

6. Did my Daddy ever teach you anything? _____

_____

7. Did my Daddy ever tell you anything about me? _____

_____

8. What is something you will always remember about him? _____

_____

9. If there was something Daddy would want me to always remember, what would it be?

_____

_____

10. Do you have a good story about Daddy? _____

_____

_____

_____

Memories From Others - Stories

Ask friends and family members to write down a
memory that they have of your Daddy.

Name: _____ Date: _____

_____

_____

_____

_____

_____

Name: _____ Date: _____

_____

_____

_____

_____

_____

Memories From Others - Stories

Name: _____ Date: _____

_____

_____

_____

_____

_____

_____

Name: _____ Date: _____

_____

_____

_____

_____

_____

_____

Memories From Others - Stories

Name: _____ Date: _____

_____

_____

_____

_____

_____

_____

Name: _____ Date: _____

_____

_____

_____

_____

_____

_____

Memories From Others - Stories

Name: _____   Date: _____

_____

_____

_____

_____

_____

Name: _____   Date: _____

_____

_____

_____

_____

_____

Memories From Others - Stories

Name: _____   Date: _____

_____

_____

_____

_____

_____

_____

_____

_____

_____

_____

_____

_____

Memories From Others - Stories

Name: _____   Date: _____

Memories From Others - Stories

Name: _____   Date: _____

Memories From Others - Stories

Name: _____   Date: _____

_____

_____

_____

_____

_____

_____

_____

_____

_____

_____

_____

Memories From Others - Stories

Name: _____   Date: _____

_____

_____

_____

_____

_____

_____

_____

_____

_____

_____

_____

_____

Dear Daddy,

Writing can really help us get out all our BIG feelings and help us feel better.

Use these next few pages to write to your Daddy anytime you want to tell him something.

You can also have someone else write the words for you.

If you enjoy writing to him, you may want to get another journal that you can keep all your feelings in one place.

If you could talk to him right now, what would you say?

Letter to Daddy

_____
Date

_____

_____

_____

_____

_____

_____

_____

_____

_____

_____

_____

_____

_____

Letter to Daddy

_____
Date

Letter to Daddy

_____
Date

Letter to Daddy

_____ **Date**

Letter to Daddy

_____
Date

_____

_____

_____

_____

_____

_____

_____

_____

_____

_____

_____

_____

_____

_____

Journaling

The following pages are for you to journal your thoughts and to draw pictures.

_____

_____

_____

_____

_____

_____

_____

_____

_____

_____

_____

_____

Please email me at KatRobBooks@gmail.com

I would love to hear your story and/or input for future memory books.

Visit www.KatRobBooks.com for information about the

<u>Memories Of... Series</u>

Memories of My Mommy (child)

Memories of My Mom (teenager/young adult)

Memories of My Mother (adult)

Memories of My Daddy (child)

Memories of My Dad (teen/young adult)

Memories of My Father (adult)

Memories of My Grandmother

Memories of My Grandfather

Memories of My Sister

Memories of My Brother

Memories of My Friend

And other versions!

Made in United States
Orlando, FL
12 June 2025

62079544R00052